Pebble®
Plus

ICE
AGE
ANIMALS

Sabertooth Cats

by Melissa Higgins

Consulting Editor: Gail Saunders-Smith, PhD

Content Consultant: Margaret M. Yacobucci, PhD
Education and Outreach Coordinator,
Paleontological Society; Associate Professor,
Department of Geology, Bowling Green State University

CAPSTONE PRESS
a capstone imprint

Pebble Plus is published by Capstone Press,
1710 Roe Crest Drive, North Mankato, Minnesota 56003
www.capstonepub.com

Library of Congress Cataloging-in-Publication Data
Higgins, Melissa, 1953– author.
Sabertooth cats / by Melissa Higgins.
pages cm.—(Pebble Plus. Ice Age Animals)
Summary: "Describes the characteristics, food, habitat, behavior, and extinction
of Ice Age sabertooth cats"—Provided by publisher.
Audience: Age 5–8.
Audience: Grades K to 3.
Includes bibliographical references and index.
ISBN 978-1-4914-2103-1 (library binding)
ISBN 978-1-4914-2321-9 (paperback)
ISBN 978-1-4914-2344-8 (eBook pdf)
1. Saber-toothed tigers—Juvenile literature. 2. Extinct mammals—Juvenile literature. I. Title.
QE882.C15H54 2015
569.74—frvdc23   2014029100

Editorial Credits
Jeni Wittrock, editor; Peggie Carley and Janet Kusmierski, designers; Wanda Winch, media
researcher; Laura Manthe, production specialist

Photo Credits
Illustrator: Jon Hughes
Shutterstock: Alex Staroseltsev, snowball, April Cat, icicles, Kotkoa, cover background, Leigh
Prather, ice crystals, pcruciatti, interior background

Note to Parents and Teachers

The Ice Age Animals set supports national science standards related to life
science. This book describes and illustrates sabertooth cats. The images support
early readers in understanding the text. The repetition of words and phrases
helps early readers learn new words. This book also introduces early readers to
subject-specific vocabulary words, which are defined in the Glossary section.
Early readers may need assistance to read some words and to use the Table of
Contents, Glossary, Read More, Internet Sites, and Index sections of the book.

Printed in China by Nordica.
0914/CA21401504
092014   008470NORDS15

Table of Contents

Ice-Age Hunter

Roar!

A sabertooth cat warns

an enemy to stay back.

Grazers look up, ready to run.

Sabertooth cats last roamed
North and South America
10,000 years ago. They lived
in grasslands and forests.
The world was cooler then.

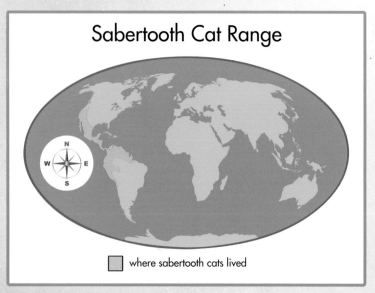

Sabertooth Cat Range

☐ where sabertooth cats lived

Big and Strong

Sabertooth cats were about 3 feet (1 meter) tall. Their strong bodies had big muscles and short tails. Females and males were the same size.

The cat's two long teeth were called canines. These sharp, 7-inch (18-centimeter) teeth could cut through tough skin.

Ambush!

The slow and heavy sabertooth did not chase prey. It hid and waited. When prey came close, pounce! The cat stabbed prey with its sharp canines.

Sabertooth cats hunted bison. They also hunted camels and horses. They could even take down young mammoths.

Sabertooth Life

Sabertooth cats were mammals. Young kittens drank their mothers' milk. Older kittens ate meat their parents killed.

Sabertooths probably lived
in groups. Healthy sabertooths
may have shared their food
with hurt sabertooths.

Around 10,000 years ago,
the earth became warmer.
Humans settled in the
sabertooths' home. Soon the
big cats became extinct.

Glossary

canine—a long, pointed tooth

extinct—no longer living; an extinct animal is one that has died out, with no more of its kind

grazer—an animal that eats grass

Ice Age—a time when much of Earth was covered in ice; the last ice age ended about 11,500 years ago

pounce—to jump on something suddenly and grab it

prey—an animal that is hunted for food

stab—to poke with something sharp

Read More

Bailey, Gerry. *Sabre-Tooth Tiger. Smithsonian Prehistoric Zone.* New York: Crabtree Publishing, 2011.

Worth, Bonnie. *Once Upon a Mastodon: All About Prehistoric Mammals. The Cat in the Hat's Learning Library.* New York: Random House, 2014.

Zabludoff, Marc. *Saber-Toothed Cat.* Prehistoric Beasts. New York: Benchmark Books, 2010.

Internet Sites

FactHound offers a safe, fun way to find Internet sites related to this book. All of the sites on FactHound have been researched by our staff.

Here's all you do:

Visit *www.facthound.com*

Type in this code: 9781491421031

Check out projects, games and lots more at
www.capstonekids.com

Index

Word Count: 176
Grade: 1
Early-Intervention Level: 16